TAP DANCING

LET'S DANCE

Tracy M. Maurer

The Rourke Press, Inc.
Vero Beach, Florida 32964

Tracy M. Maurer, author of the Dance Series, specializes in non-fiction and business writing. She has previously worked with several educational organizations on various writing projects, including creating classroom workbooks for elementary students. Tracy's most recently published hard cover book focused on the city of Macon, Georgia. A graduate of the University of Minnesota - Minneapolis School of Journalism, she now lives in Park Falls, Wisconsin, with her husband Mike.

PHOTO CREDITS
© Timothy L. Vacula: cover, title page, pages 8, 10, 13, 17; © Lois M. Nelson: pages 4, 12, 15, 18; © Michael Le Poer Trench: page 7; © Michal Daniel: page 21

With appreciation to Jane Madison, The Madison Studio, Macon, GA; Marv Miller, The Dance Shoppe, Minneapolis, MN; Merle Frimark Associates, New York, NY, for *Riverdance*; The Public Theater, New York, NY, for *Bring In 'Da Noise, Bring In 'Da Funk*

EDITORIAL SERVICES:
Penworthy Learning Systems and Lois M. Nelson

Library of Congress Cataloging-in-Publication Data

Maurer, Tracy M, 1965-
    Tap Dancing / Tracy M. Maurer
        p. cm. — (Let's dance)
    Includes index
    Summary: Discusses the history, techniques, and styles of this American dance, where to see tap dancing, and how performances by such dancers as Savion Glover have helped to renew tap's popularity in the 1990s.
    ISBN 1-57103-172-3
    1. Tap Dancing—Juvenile literature. [1. Tap Dancing] I. Title II. Series: Maurer, Tracy, 1965-   Let's dance.
GV1794.M29 1997
792.7—dc21   97-8392
                                                    CIP
                                                    AC

TABLE OF CONTENTS

MOTION AND SOUND

Say "digga-digga-DOG" four times the same way. Do you hear the rhythm?

You can see tap dancing and hear its **rhythmic patterns** (RITH mic PAT ernz). Tap dancers use their feet like drums to create rhythmic patterns.

Tap dancers first learn to make basic rhythmic patterns, or moves, with their feet. Then they link these moves together in the steps that create exciting tap **routines** (roo TEENZ).

Tap dancers learn a new tap routine by watching their teacher.

AN AMERICAN DANCE

Tap dancing began in America in the 1840s. Slave owners banned drumming among the African people, so the slaves clapped their hands and tapped their feet to make the **percussive** (per KUS iv) sounds. They mixed their African dances with the European "step dancing" and clog dancing, which often used noisy wooden shoes.

Early tap dancers performed flat-footed steps with relaxed arms. In time, they added arm movements, **acrobatics** (AK ruh BAT iks), and even ballet steps.

The world-famous show Riverdance *features Irish music, dances, and songs; the fast footwork of Irish dances influenced American tap dancing.*

USING TAP DANCE SKILLS

Today many children and adults learn tap dancing for fun and exercise. Tap dancing builds aerobic fitness, muscle control, and rhythmic movement.

Actors, singers, and dancers of all kinds take tap lessons to improve their performances. They may need tap skills to act in musicals, plays, and films.

Gymnasts and figure skaters often learn tap dancing to bring new ideas to their routines.

As part of their physical training, tap dancers must do stretching exercises before every class, rehearsal, or performance.

LEARNING TO TAP

Tap dancers usually take lessons at dance studios. Classes begin with stretching exercises to warm up the muscles. After reviewing the steps they already know, students then add new moves to their **repertoire** (REP er TWAHR).

Teachers listen for crisp, clean tap sounds and watch for proper arm, hand, leg, and foot positions.

Skilled dancers **improvise** (IM pruh VYZ) their own tap steps. They can also "borrow" steps, or try to copy certain tap sounds, by watching and hearing other dancers.

A teacher shows a student the correct foot positions in a new routine.

Instructors often walk around the studio to listen for each child's tapping sounds and to show proper dance movements.

During the 1920s, uniform costumes became popular; today dancers may use hats and canes that look like those of early tappers.

PRACTICE EVERY DAY

Tap dance students should practice every day, even if they go to class only once a week.

When students know enough steps to make routines, the teacher may host a **recital** (ri SYT uhl). The dancers at the recital may perform solos or in groups.

A special dress rehearsal lets the dancers practice their routines dressed in costumes.

Many tappers learn the foot movements of a routine before they add the hand and arm movements.

TAPPERS AND HOOFERS

Tap dancers have created different styles of tap dancing over the years. The most famous style, classical tap, uses upper-body movements in steps that blend tap with ballet or ballroom dancing.

Tappers (TAP erz) often perform classical tap. These tap dancers seem to float on their feet, smoothly moving their arms and hands.

Hoofers (HOOF erz) focus on percussive footwork with very little upper-body movement. They often perform rhythm tap, using every part of their shoes to make drum-like sounds.

Tappers often use ballet and other dance forms to make their routines look more graceful.

TWO SHOES, FOUR TAPS

Tap dancers make most of their sounds with metal taps on the heels and toes of their shoes. Dancers can make extra noise with metal "jingle taps" on their heels. Each jingle tap holds a sturdy, metal ring inside that jingles with each heel tap.

Soft-shoe (SOFT SHOO) dancers do not wear metal taps. Soft-soled leather shoes create the rhythmic "shushing" in this slower style of tap. Early soft-shoe dancers poured sand on the stage to accent the sound.

In the early 1900s dancers began wearing shoes with metal taps on the heels and toes instead of shoes with wooden soles and heels; metal makes sharper sounds than wood.

TAPPING MUSIC

Jazz music and tap dancing took over American stages in the mid-1920s. Tap dancers often performed to this new music.

Now tap dancers perform with all types of music—or without any music at all. Some hoofers find rhythms in the everyday sounds around them. Savion Glover, a famous tap dancer of the 1990s, brought the "music" of the streets to the stage. His athletic, hip-hop tap style started a new era in tap dancing.

Bring In 'Da Noise, Bring In 'Da Funk, *the hit Broadway show, features the street-smart tap routines created by Savion Glover (shown right).*

WHERE TO SEE TAP DANCING

From the 1920s until the 1950s, nearly every kind of traveling show and musical film had tap dancing in it. The movie *Tap* and the Broadway show *Bring In 'Da Noise, Bring In 'Da Funk* helped make tap dancing popular again in the 1990s.

If you can, attend a live performance at a dance school recital or theater. Many video stores also carry tap dancing movies. Visit the library to learn more about tap dancing and discover the thrilling sights and sounds of this American dance.

Glossary

acrobatics (AK ruh BAT iks) — gymnastic or tumbling movements, such as the splits

hoofers (HOOF erz) — professional dancers, especially tap dancers who focus on percussive footwork with very little upper-body movement

improvise (IM pruh VYZ) — to make up something, like a dance step or a song

percussive (per KUS iv) — a drum-like sound

recital (ri SYT uhl) — a show with solo or group performances

repertoire (REP er TWAHR) — the set of steps or routines a dancer has learned well enough to perform

rhythmic patterns (RITH mic PAT ernz) — the basic moves and sounds that tap dancers make by tapping their heels and toes

routines (roo TEENZ) — the sets of dance steps or other movements that make up performances

soft-shoe (SOFT SHOO) — a slower style of tap dancing without taps on the shoes that creates a rhythmic "shushing"

tappers (TAP erz) — professional dancers, especially tap dancers who blend footwork with smooth upper-body movements

INDEX